CONTEMPORARY ARTIST 2024

Tim Saunders

Creative Coverage

COVERAGE

Copyright © 2024 Contributors

All rights reserved

No part of this book may be reproduced, or stored in a retrieval system, or transmitted in any form or by any means, electronic, mechanical, photocopying, recording, or otherwise, without express written permission of the publisher.

Cover image: Jane Goodall portrait by John Atkinson
Cover design: Creative Coverage

CONTENTS

Title Page
Copyright
Foreword
John Atkinson — 1
Joanna Commings — 4
Rowena Comrie — 5
Dominic Fondé — 6
Sue Goodchild — 10
Jacqui Harrison — 11
Barbara Mackie — 12
Roberta Mason — 14
Andrew Matheson — 16
L. Paul Matthews — 18
Eric Pentecost — 20
Sarah Pye — 22
Ingrid Skoglund — 24
Brian Steventon — 25
About — 27
Also available — 29

FOREWORD

It's been another challenging year all round and the art market does not escape. A year that has seen a change of government in the UK, a change that is yet to bring stability it would seem. Of course America is also going through change as President Biden prepares to leave the White House to be replaced by Donald Trump, who will be President for the next four years. We can only hope that he will play his part in bringing peace to an unhappy world. When consumers feel happier, they will spend more and the art world will regain its momentum.

Despite this difficult backdrop, thank goodness that artists and makers continue to produce some excellent work. Theirs is a vital role in communicating beyond words.

Caroline and I are privileged to work with a number of hugely talented artists and makers at Creative Coverage and this issue of Contemporary Artist showcases what some of them have been up to during 2024. There's a lot of good news, thanks to their efforts.

Tim Saunders
Editor

JOHN ATKINSON

Ninety years of hope: A portrait of Jane Goodall

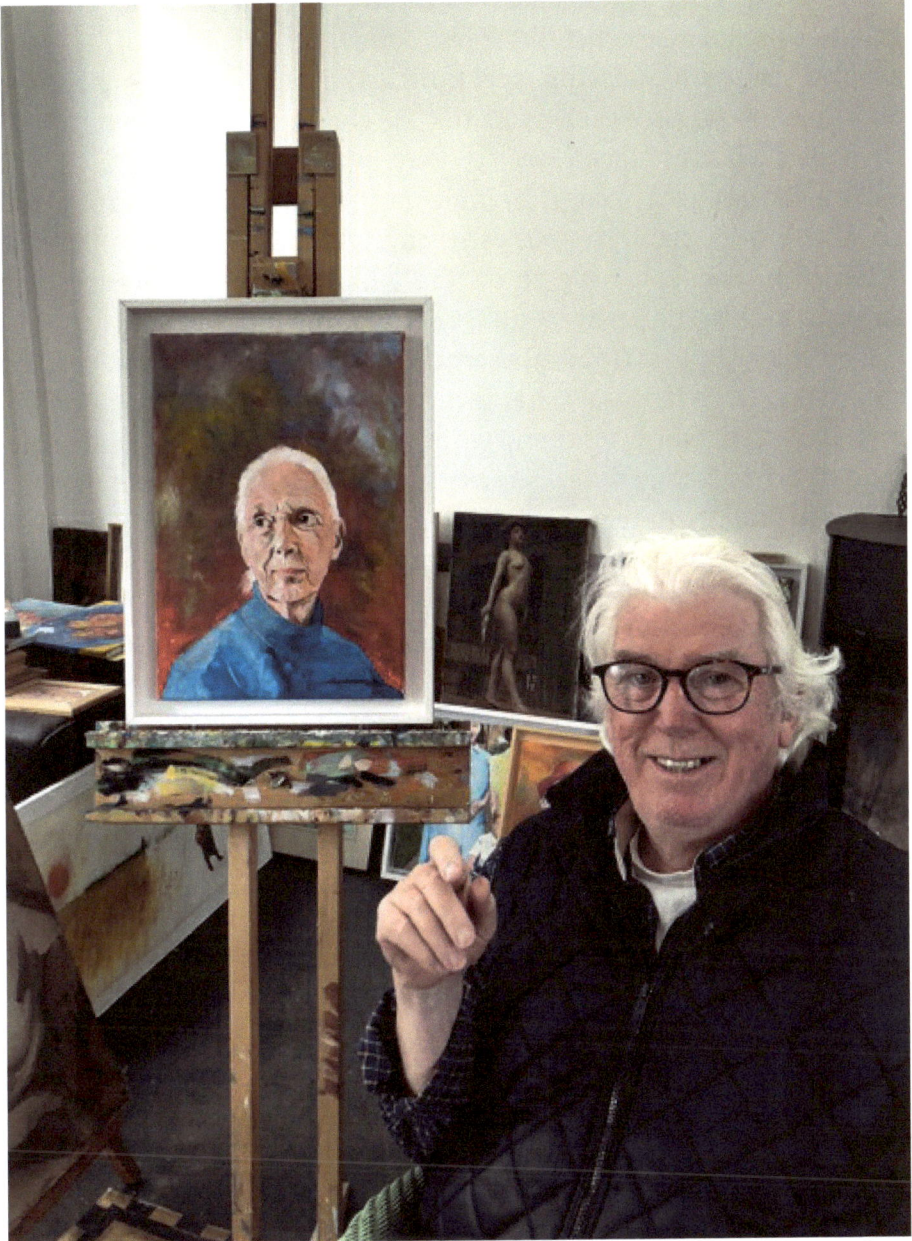

"I have just completed a portrait of Jane Goodall to celebrate her

90th birthday," says John Atkinson.

Dame Jane Morris Goodall DBE is an English primatologist and anthropologist. She is considered the world's foremost expert on chimpanzees after years studying the social and family interactions of wild chimpanzees. Today, Dr Jane Goodall travels around the world, writing, speaking and spreading hope through action, encouraging each of us to "use the gift of our life to make the world a better place".

"You cannot get through a single day without having an impact on the world around you," she says. "What you do makes a difference, and you have to decide what kind of difference you want to make. The greatest danger to our future is apathy."

Everyday, Dr Jane Goodall exemplifies the difference one person can make. Over the years, her groundbreaking research at Gombe has attracted many women, who were almost absent from the field of primatology when she began. Today, women lead the field of long-term primate behavioural studies around the world.

She also inspires hundreds of thousands of young people to take action in their own lives and communities through the Roots & Shoots youth programme. Now 100 countries are strong and growing thanks to Roots & Shoots, which is an unprecedented multiplying force in conservation, giving young people the knowledge and confidence to act on their beliefs and make a difference by being part of something bigger than themselves.

John took the liberty of painting Jane's portrait, a quick oil sketch on canvas, as a birthday gift. "What I tried to achieve within the painting was to show her determination and the hard work she has done in the past years." He has called the painting Ninety Years of Hope. "I hope I have captured her beauty and honesty, with love and admiration. It may look a little hard and unflattering but I didn't want to make it smiley, smiley, if you know what I mean. I think the expression and colours resonate hope and the natural world she inhabits. I think it captures her stoic determination to make a difference."

Jane's response at seeing the portrait: "I am overwhelmed that you have painted a portrait of me. Not only do I like it – it is one of only a VERY few that I like. Usually, I dislike them intensely, but yours makes me look as I often feel."

There's praise indeed. Congratulations John.

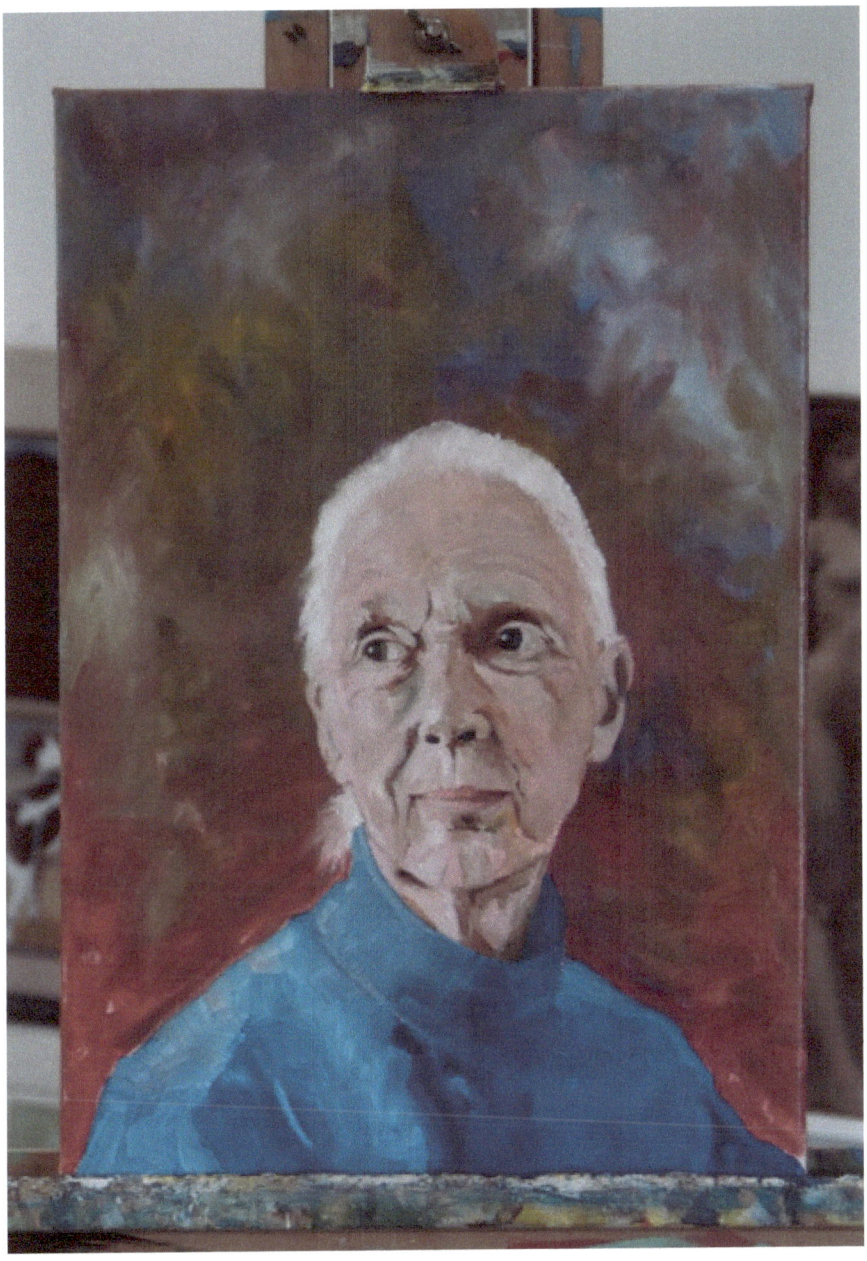

JOANNA COMMINGS

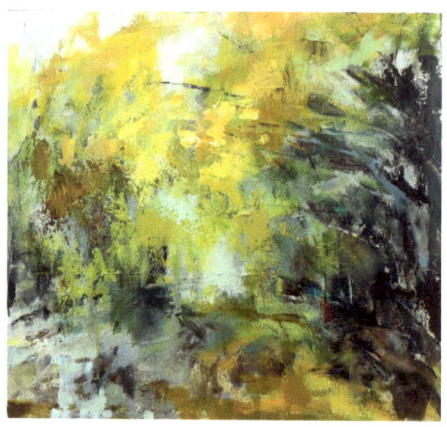

Joanna's father was an artist and she has been painting and drawing all her life, though she has done a number of courses over the years. Her working practice is to go out into the countryside and take many panoramic photos of a selected subject, from which she will work up her paintings in comfort back in the studio. Working in acrylics because she loves their versatility, Joanna almost always paints on canvas.

"I will begin with a loose wash and then build up more and more layers, continually reassessing and allowing the paint to suggest and dictate where that will enhance the image," she says. "What inspires me is the natural landscape, whether field or forest, cliffs or canal, it is mood and atmosphere that I wish to reflect. Sunlight through foliage, clouds, reflections or movement of water, effects of season and weather."

Joanna spent many years living on the north Cornish coast and still returns there for inspiration. Her work is exhibited in galleries throughout the south west.

ROWENA COMRIE

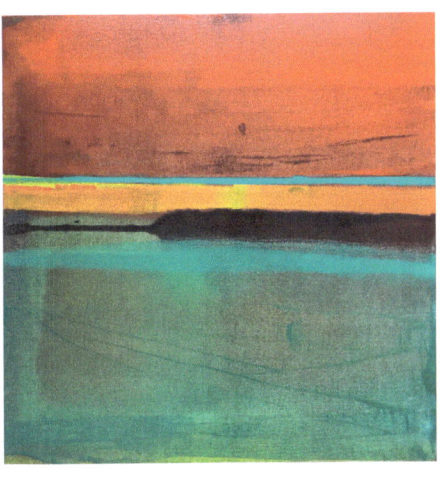

Rowena Comrie has worked as a professional artist for the past 35 years in Scotland, UK where she now works from a WASPS (Workshop & Studio Provision Scotland), studio at the Dovehill Studios in Glasgow's Gallowgate.

Rowena was born in Southend-on-Sea, Essex and in 1982 completed her degree in Fine Art at Reading University where she embraced expressionist colour field painting with confidence and passion. "I continue to develop this dramatic and emotive painting style, making these works from a specific aesthetic point that personally expresses sublime elements of human experiences," says Rowena.

"Over many years I have refined and developed my technique, a process that continues to challenge and intrigue." Rowena has received awards from Creative Scotland, the Hope Scott Trust and Paisley Art Institute, among others. She is a professional elected member of the Society of Scottish Artists and served as President of the Scottish Artists Union between 2011 and 2014. Her work is held in many collections including Aberdeen Art Gallery & Museum and the New Hall Art Collection, Cambridge.

DOMINIC FONDÉ

Five portraits in glass by Japan based Dominic Fondé have been added to the permanent glass collection at the Victoria and Albert Museum in London.

1. Pandemic self-portrait
2. Pandemic Portrait of Yoshiko Sakai-Fondé
35. Pandemic Portrait of Kaori Shimizu
36. Pandemic Portrait of Okasan Shimizu San
37. Pandemic Portrait of Shimizu Family

"I've been picked up as a partner artist of a company here in Japan called Sonidori," says Dominc.
  "They have a page listed on their website through which people can purchase or commission work from me.
  "Everything Sonidori does is bird related and as their logo is a kingfisher they have specifically requested kingfisher's for this first round of works."

CONTEMPORARY ARTIST 2024

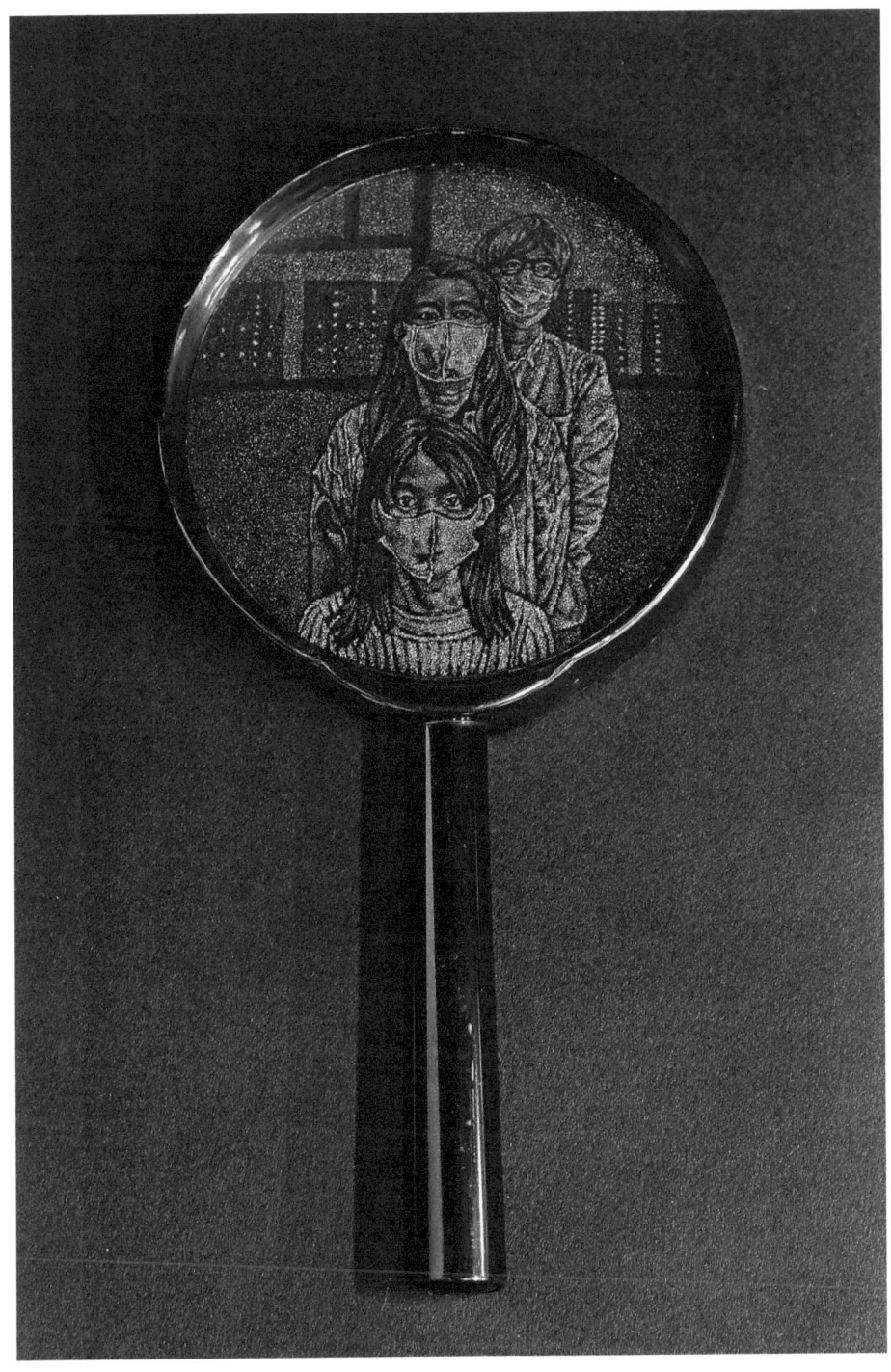

EDITED BY TIM SAUNDERS

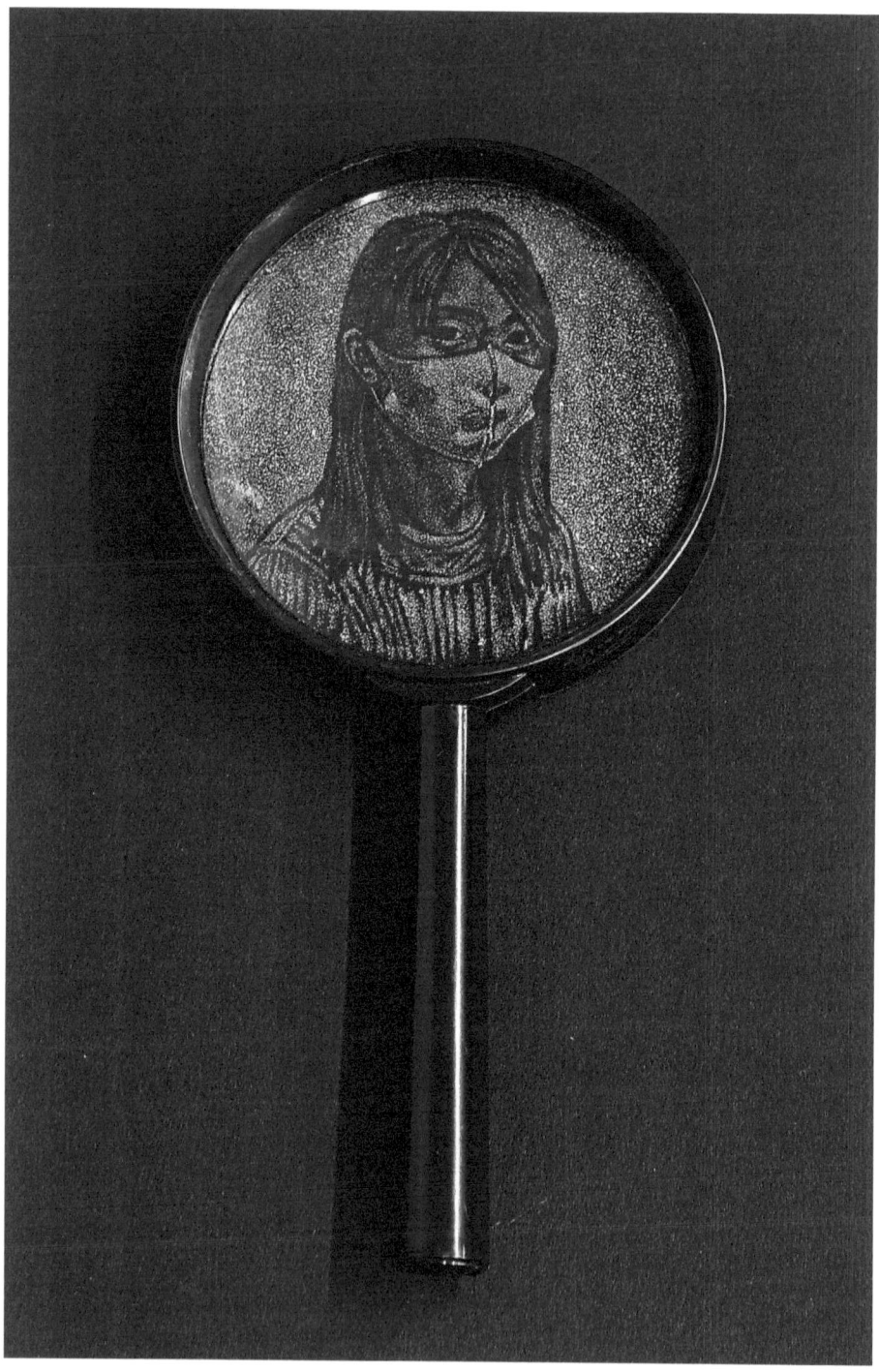

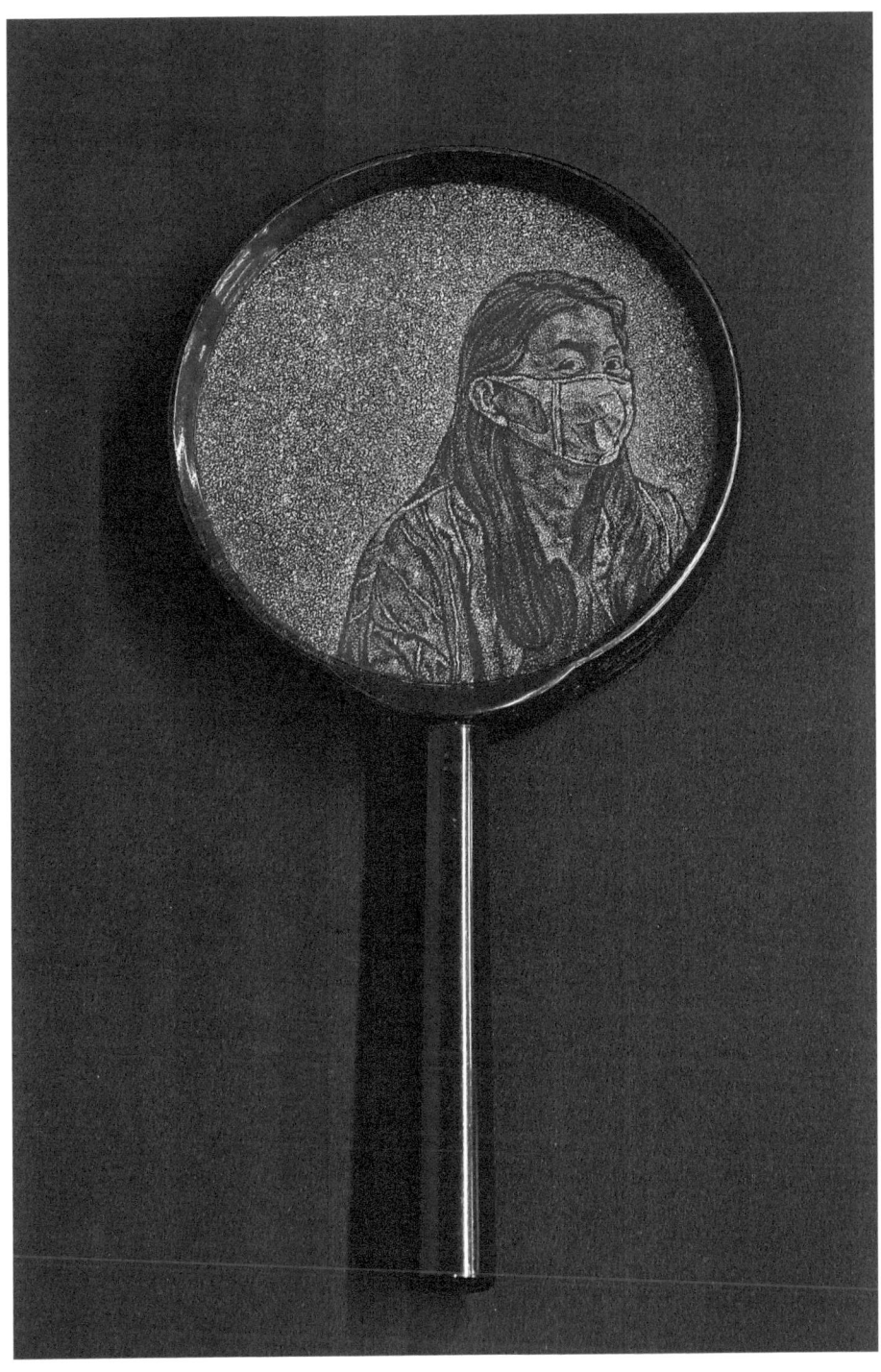

SUE GOODCHILD

Whatever the time of year there is always inspiration in the garden for this artist and gardener.
During this year Creative Coverage has published Sue's A Year in My Garden series of books, which are available in all good bookshops and online.

A Year in My Garden
The Artist and the Gardener: Autumn

By Sue Goodchild

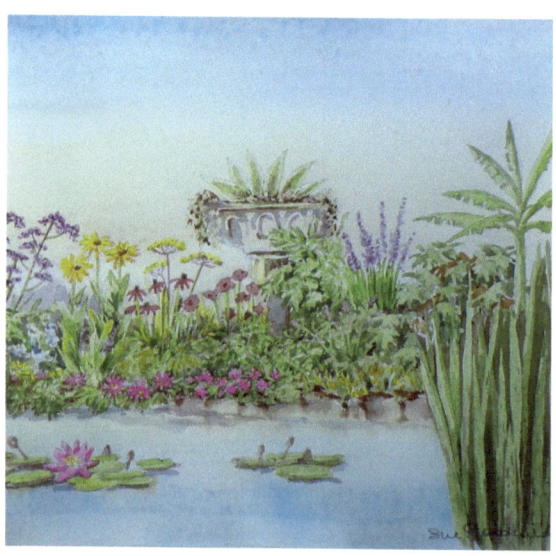

JACQUI HARRISON

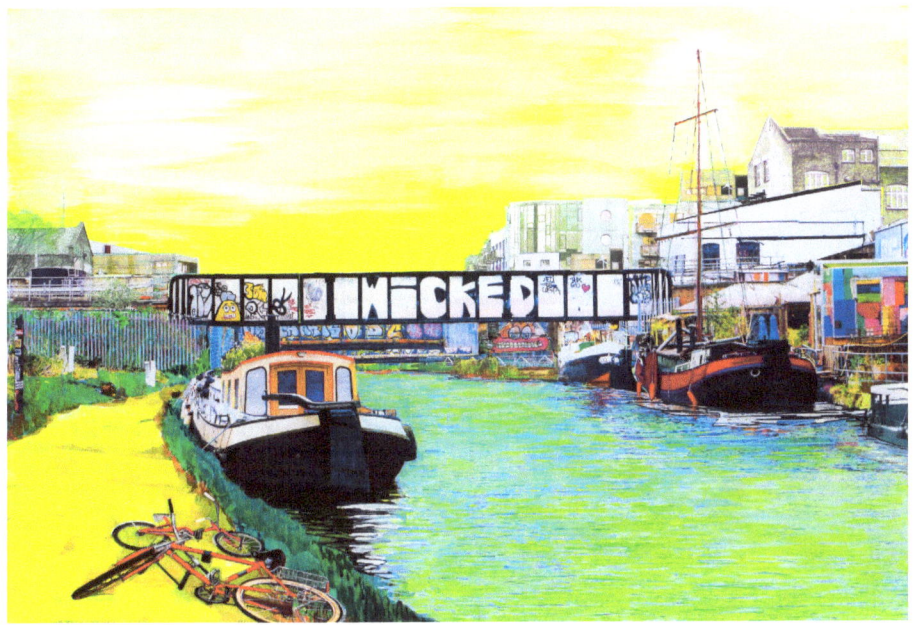

This summer Jacqui participated in an exhibition about hobbies put on by Artangel, called Come As You Really Are.

"My contribution was my enormously extravagant Sindy dolls house, from where I am certain so much of my creativity stems."

BARBARA MACKIE

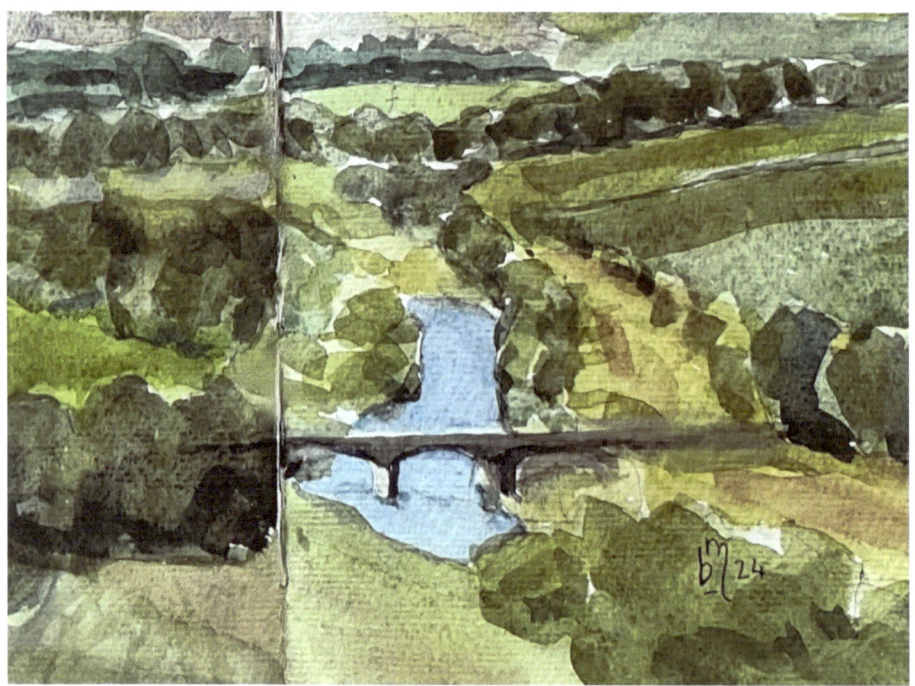

Barbara is inspired by the physical environment and the importance that time, place and memory play in its appeal.

"During 2024 I have been working in watercolour out of doors and studying subject matter by drawing in and out of the studio," says Barbara.

"Going forward I will be developing some work that explores bonds that form and thread through our lives; that navigate both family and professional lives. It is a slow burn project as 'the Joy of Reunion'."

Currently, Barbara is focussing on watercolour and line drawing as distinct disciplines, both of which she enjoys very much.

The recent watercolours were painted out of doors and studio work is also going on.

Last summer she was studying a newly harvested sweetcorn

in all its splendour.

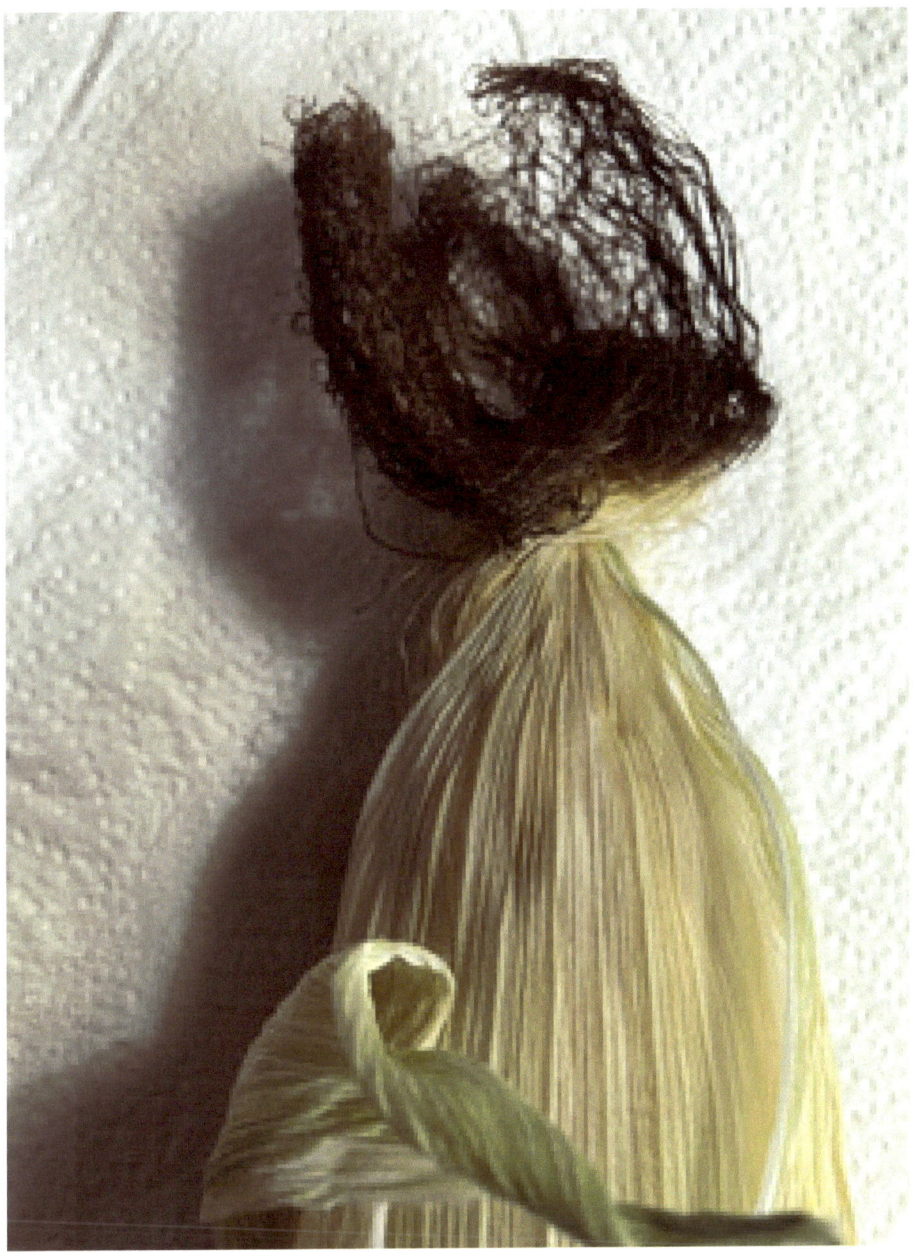

ROBERTA MASON

"Passionate about our oceans, my work often explores perspectives around our relationship with the environment," says Roberta. "My current work is inspired by ocean phenomena and my research has led me to study the formation of waves and bubbles as well as the wonderful world of marine creatures.

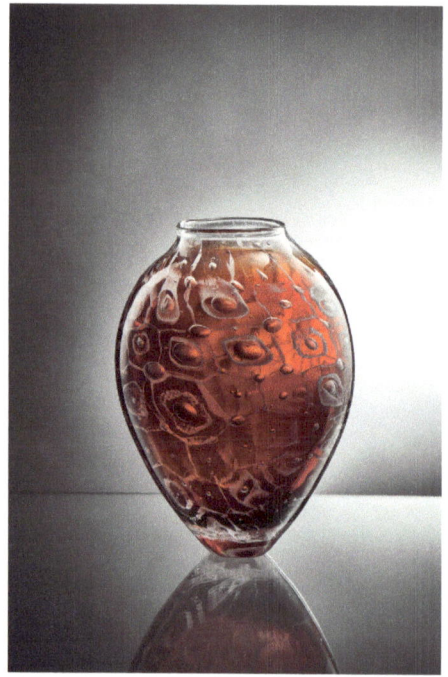

"The forms I make are my re-imagining and my aim is for them to be interesting enough to engage people to find out more. In the words of Aristotle, 'Wonder is the source of our desire for knowledge'. I hope this is the case. My aim is to promote engagement and hopefully with it, awareness, understanding and the desire to protect and respect our marine environments."

Roberta uses traditional glass techniques, in a non-traditional way, to create unique, sculptural work and installations. Glass enables her to capture a snapshot of life in a way no other material can; the glass interacts with light in its own unique way to give the work a life of its own. She has been exhibiting her work since 2010 and has an MA in Ceramics and Glass from the Royal College of Art. Memberships include the Contemporary Glass Society, the Scottish Glass Society and Handmade in Britain.

Roberta's work is available for sale in the Creative Coverage Artfinder gallery.

CONTEMPORARY ARTIST 2024

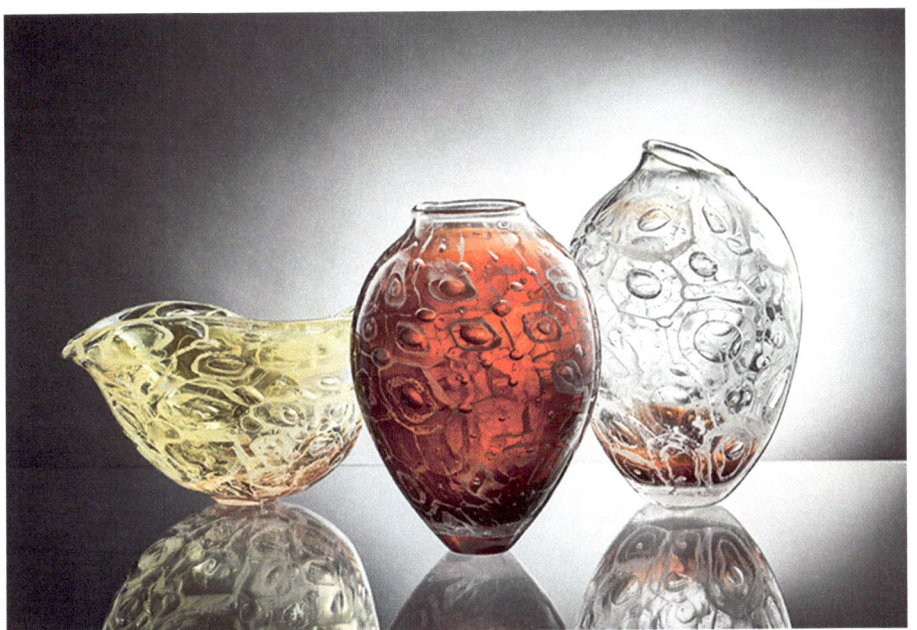

ANDREW MATHESON

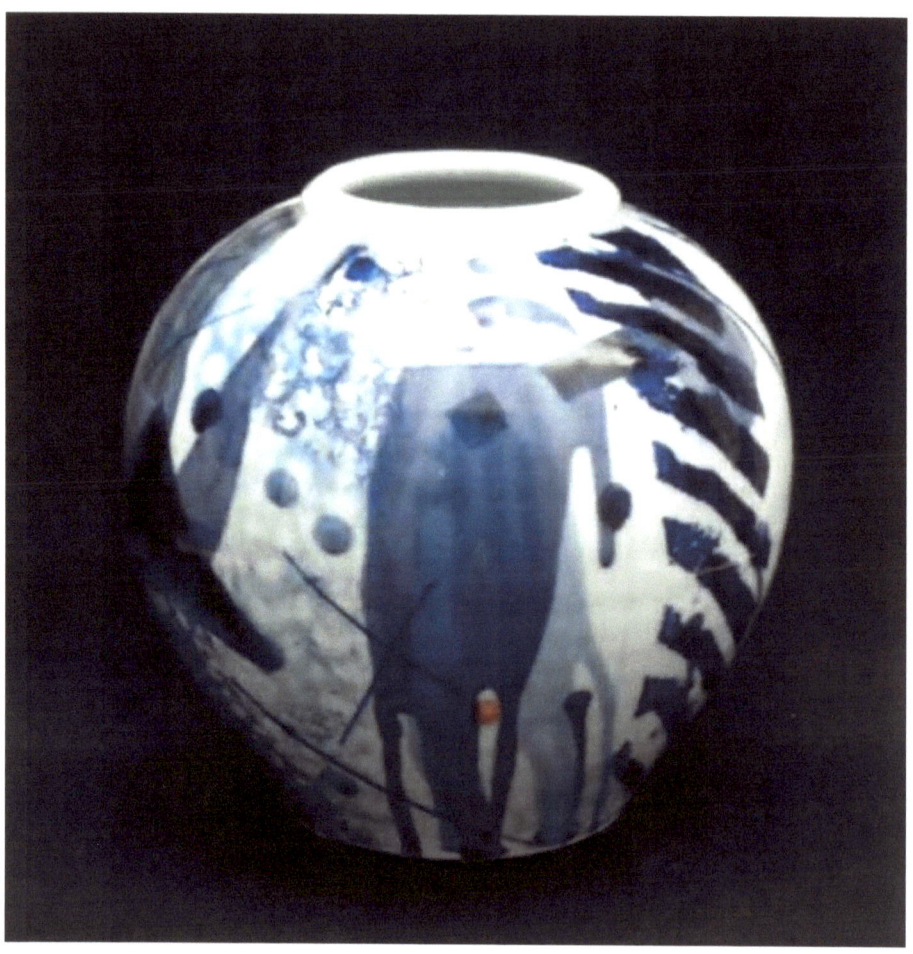

In October, alumnus of Gray's School of Art, Andrew Matheson, held a Journey through cobalt blue workshop at Gray's School of Art in Aberdeen. Afterwards there was an exhibition and evening with Andrew at the Scottish Ceramics Gallery.

The wheel forms the basis of most of Staffordshire based Andrew Matheson's work.

Skills learnt through repetition throwing and the discipline required help to inform and develop the individual pieces. "I enjoy and get great satisfaction from all stages of the making right through to the final firing," says Andrew. "All glazes are made by me from research and experimentation and trials of glazes based on oriental tradition. Together with the reduction technique this helps to achieve a distinct range of glazes. Many of the landscape forms and panels incorporate more slabbing hand building techniques with areas of texture to achieve the desired result. The work can be classified into three distinct styles: thrown functional and individual pieces, blue and white ware and landscape ware. Customers include HRH Prince of Wales who purchased two of Andrew's large stoneware bowls.

Andrew's work is available for sale in the Creative Coverage Artfinder gallery.

L. PAUL MATTHEWS

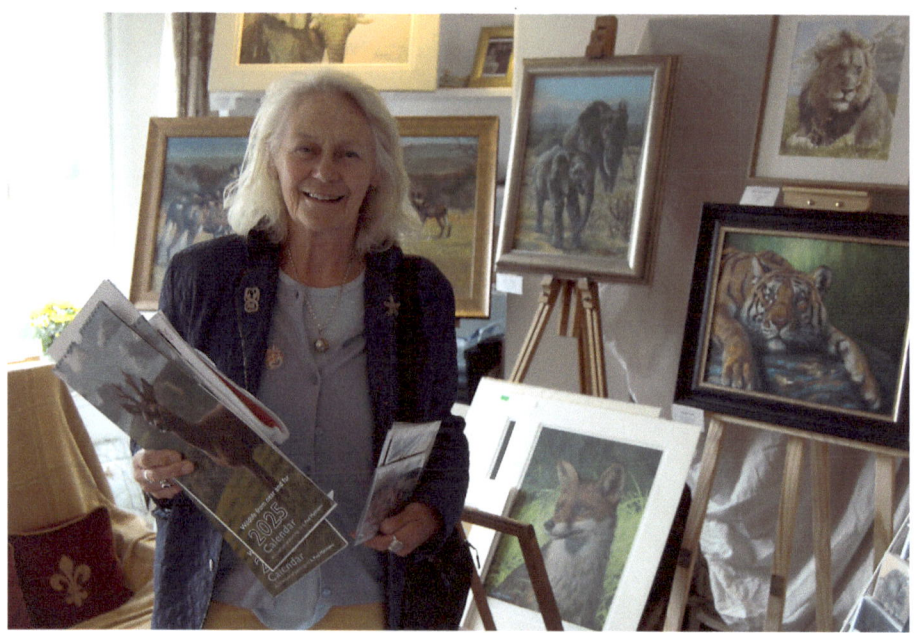

Jan Kerr with some of Paul's calendars and cards

A couple of times a year - typically in May and November - Paul opens his house in Dorset to art lovers. It's an increasingly popular event with the local community.

After painting and drawing since childhood, in August 2011 Paul chose a career as a professional artist painting wildlife and portraiture from his home in rural Dorset. Paul paints contemporary wildlife paintings where the subject takes centre stage and the mood is set by light and shade. References are collected from life by sketching and photographing in the field both at home and abroad. Recently Paul travelled to the Okavango Delta in North Botswana and has previously visited Kenya and Tanzania. The wildlife of Dorset has moved to the fore in recent years, especially due to travel restrictions but also being freed up for viewing more wildlife locally. In the summer of 2012 Paul's work attracted wide acclaim when he was a finalist in the David Shepherd Foundation's competition for Wildlife Artist of the Year.

His picture The Passenger, selected ahead of thousands of entries from all over the world received the Public's choice award at The Mall Galleries, London. Almost simultaneously Paul was in the final of the BBC Wildlife Artist of the Year competition, receiving runner up in the Frozen Planet section with his polar bear portrait. This was the fourth year Paul was shortlisted for the final of the BBC competition since its inception in 2008. You can see Paul's work online, at various galleries across Dorset and beyond. He also runs workshops and gives public demonstrations to art clubs.

ERIC PENTECOST

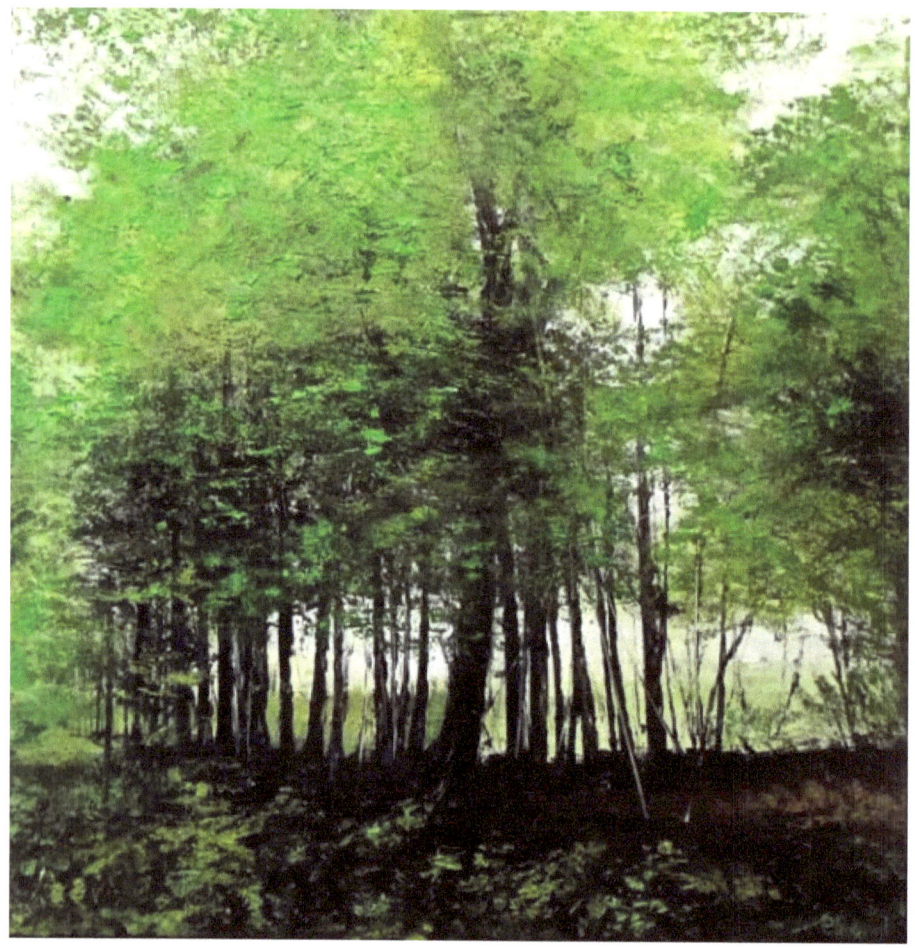

"I have sold some work this year mainly from the studio but I had another good Open Studio sale," says Eric.

Born in Brighton, Sussex in 1951, Eric received an art education at West Sussex College of Art and Design. "I continued with my art through the years on a spare time basis and settled down with my wife Sally in the West Country in the late 1970s and started selling artwork at local exhibitions around Bristol and Bath," he says.

In 2000, Eric gained a number of important painting

commissions which rekindled his passion as an artist. In 2006 he completed a study in life drawing at the Bristol Academy of Art and in 2007 he moved to Cornwall with Sally and now lives just outside St. Just on the wild and windy Penwith Peninsular.

"I have held a number of successful exhibits in Cornwall, Brittany, the Algarve and Guernsey and have sold artwork at a number of art shows in London, Edinburgh, York and Worcester. I am a landscape artist although my main interest is in the detail of the landscape. When painting outside I can be found on the edge or at the bottom of the sea cliffs, in among the hedgerows and searching the commons for prehistoric sites of our secret landscape. I revel in nature's strong sunlight and wild winds, trying to capture plant life at its best. Although I revel in strong sunlight and natures forces, I am now challenged by the darkness and damp environs of our local mines."

SARAH PYE

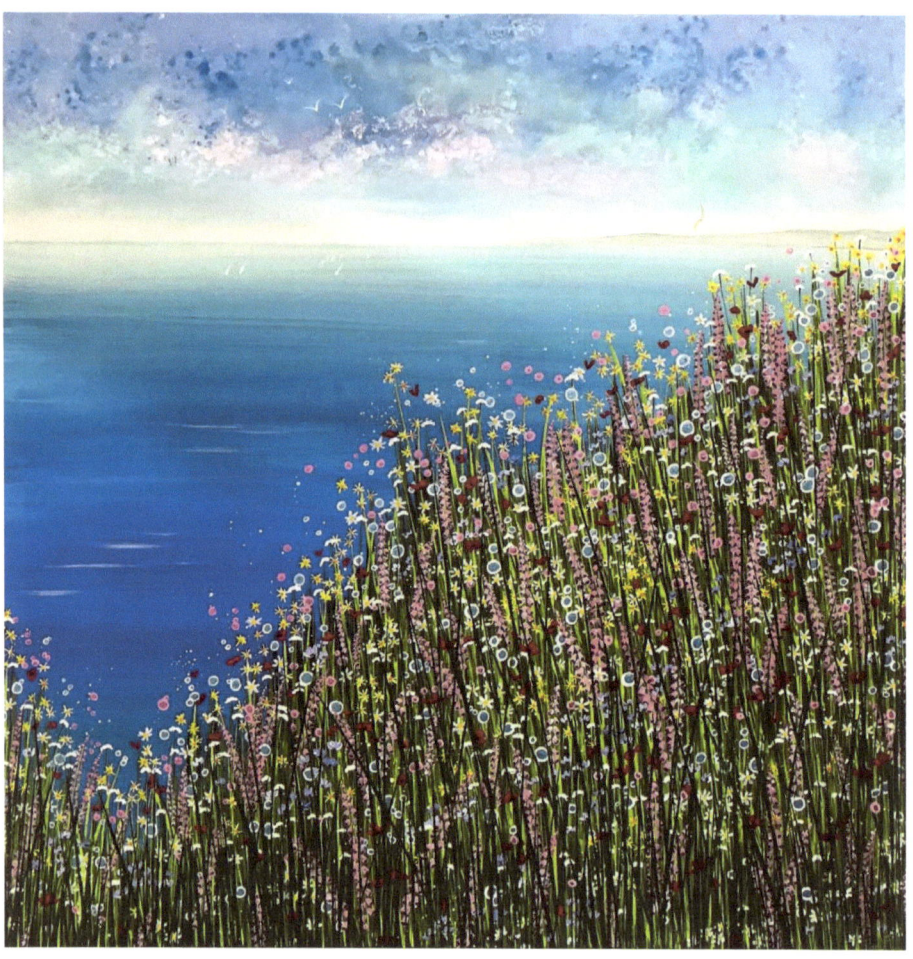

An extremely proactive member of Creative Coverage, Sarah Pye must exhibit more than 12 times a year. Recently, she had her biggest solo exhibition at Goring Village Hall in Henley.
Creative Coverage designed, hosts and regularly updates Sarah's website.

Other highlights this year for Sarah have been a question and answer in conversation with the cheese and wine community at a local gallery and her solo show at Marylebone Gallery in London.

CONTEMPORARY ARTIST 2024

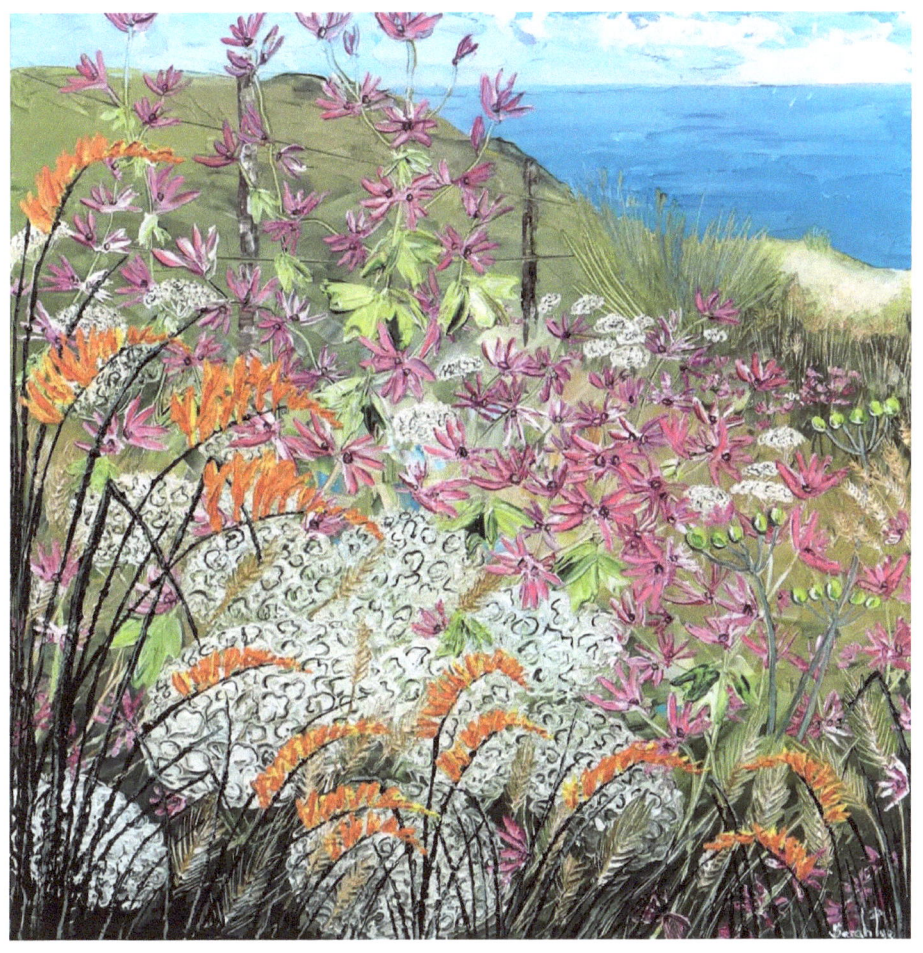

INGRID SKOGLUND

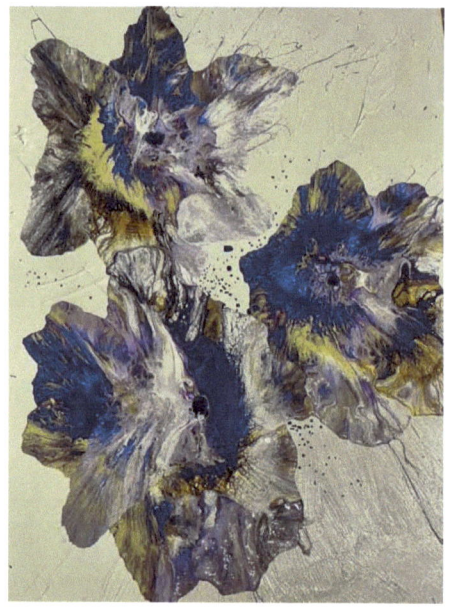

Currently an exhibiting member of Guildford Art Society, Village Artists and West Surrey Artists. Artwork exhibited in London and the south – on occasion with The Royal Watercolour Society at The Bankside Gallery, The Gosport Open and frequently at Denbies Art Gallery, Dorking. Ingrid works unconventionally with various media to produce unexpected and unpredictable effects. I rarely use a brush and am currently working with the toxic fumes of alcohol ink and isopropyl although the beautiful translucent effects are worth it. A photo of the work just can't capture it so if you like the image – the real thing is even better – just beautiful. Ingrid also often works with acrylic and silicone oil – pushing the mix around with a hot hairdryer and finishing off with a blow torch. She doesn't do cards or prints and she can't replicate a piece of work.

BRIAN STEVENTON

Brian works from the life model and plein air and uses the sketch book extensively. He models the abstract from the reality, expressiveness is crucial to progress his work. He works in oils, acrylic, gouache, watercolour and mixed media. Drawing is the backbone to what Brian does. He is an elected member of the Royal Birmingham Society of Artists.

Title: Fishing by the allotment
Med: Acrylic
Size: 47cms x 36 cms

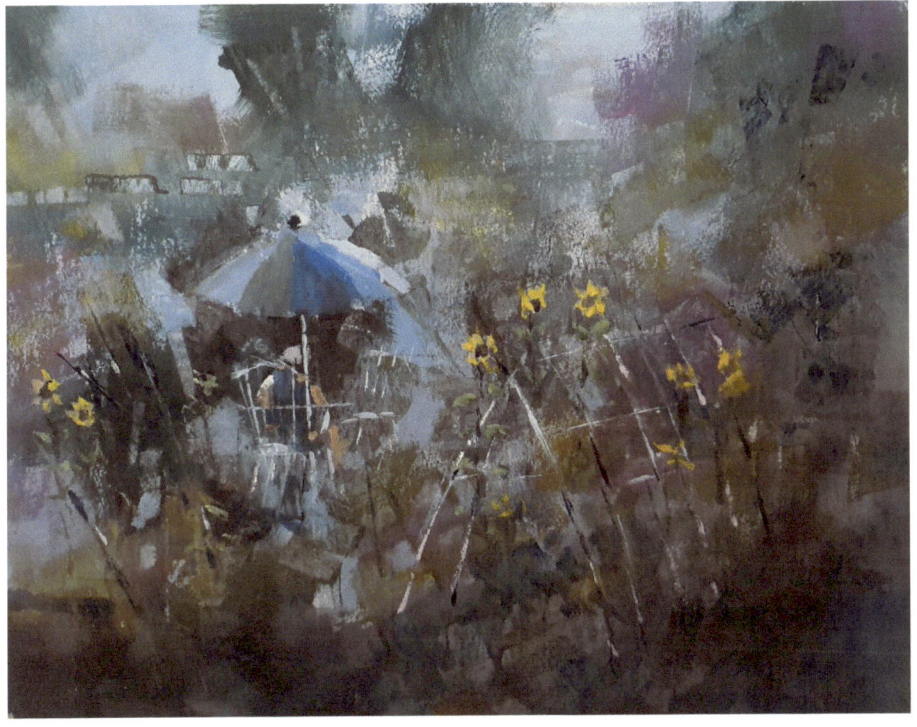

Title: Cyclamen
Med: Gouache
Size: 40cms x 40 cms

EDITED BY TIM SAUNDERS

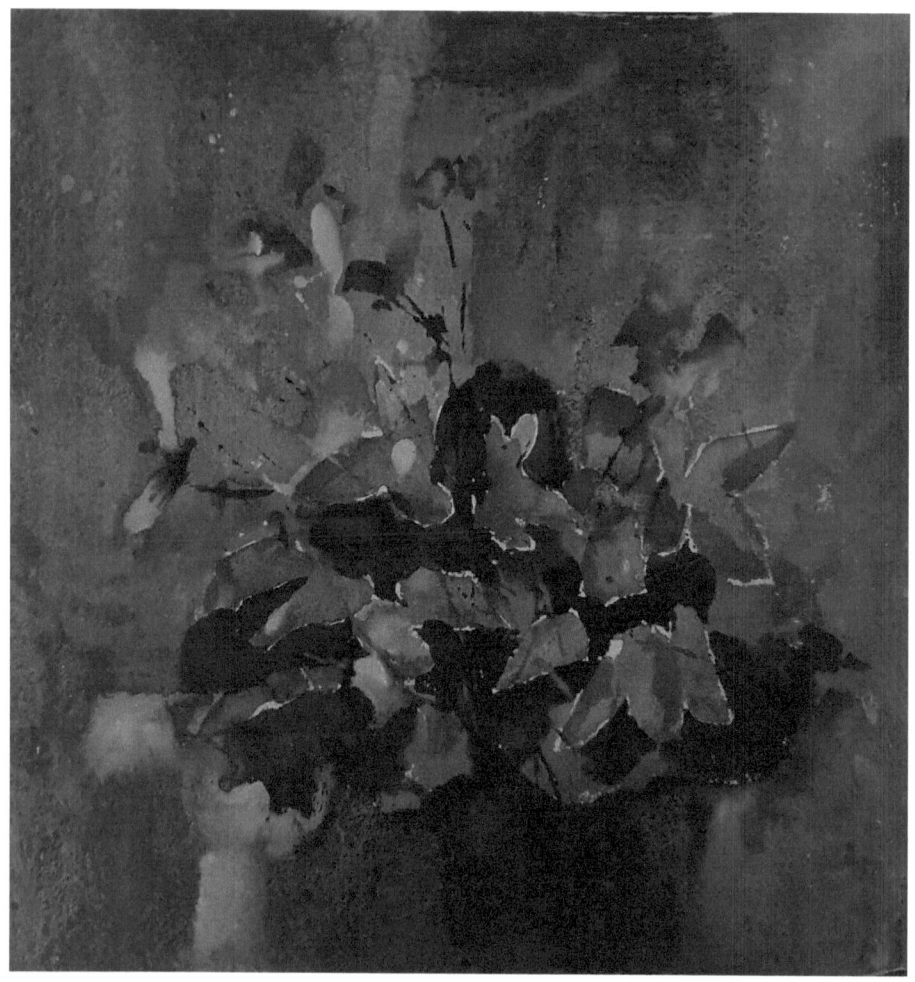

ABOUT

Creative Coverage is the marketing solution for successful professional artists and craftspeople, who are selected on merit. We also handle the marketing for galleries and arts organisations. Networking and collaborating, we make considered approaches for our members and provide time-saving services. With an excellent track record for delivering results, Creative Coverage provides opportunities that introduce artists to new audiences, helping them to become even more successful.

creativecoverage.co.uk

ALSO AVAILABLE

Celebrating Art 2024
A Year in My Garden series by Sue Goodchild
The Path Less Trodden by Don McNeil
The Path Less Trodden (Again) by Don McNeil

www.creativecoverage.co.uk

www.ingramcontent.com/pod-product-compliance
Lightning Source LLC
Chambersburg PA
CBHW040341220526
45473CB00009B/2753